Growing

Herbs

Table of Contents

Introduction

Since time unknown, plants have been a very important part of our lives. We have needed plants to fulfil various day to day needs and for our continued existence. Thus, mankind has learnt how to cultivate plants and also how to maintain them. Through the years this has led to us bettering at the art of growing these plants. We have learned how to make use of various plants for food as well as medicine. Humankind started off by growing plants for their survival but in today's times plants are grown mainly for improving our lifestyle.

Have you considered improving your lifestyle and overall quality of health by growing a small herb garden for yourself? Herbs are the most valuable and popular forms of plants today. The main reason for this is since history has begun or even before that, herbs have been used in various ways. Herbs are used to give a distinct flavour to your food, they add a special aroma in your environment, they are used as medicines for many ailments and they add colour to your garden.

When you read this article you will realize that growing herbs takes minimum efforts. You can easily grow mint, rosemary, coriander, parsley etc. in your backyard or on your terrace. With a little sunshine, some good soil that drains well, good fertilizer and regular watering, you can work wonders. As kids, I remember, my mother used to just call out for us and ask us to get a stalk of celery, coriander or mint growing in one of the pots in our backyard. In today's age when cities are losing their gardens and parks and are becoming more of a concrete jungle, having your own herb garden really helps. This article is for those who are interested in growing their own herbs. You will comprehend in this article that herbs grow easily and with minimal care.

Grow them in the ground or grow them in containers. They will flourish and spread out.

Whether you are a busy professional or a home maker, whether you have a balcony or not, this article will guide you towards growing herbs and you will be amazed with the way herbs contribute to our overall quality of health. Moreover many of the herbs will also add a lot of colour to your surroundings.

Every recipe gets a special flavour when herbs are added. Today dried herbs are available in the market but there is nothing like fresh green herbs and the only way to get fresh green herbs is to grow it yourself. Growing herbs can be fun! Grow them, attend to them, watch them flower and use them in your lovely salads or to decorate your window sill. Do you want to do all of this? Go on and read this article and follow it closely. At the end of it you will definitely be enthralled at how rewarding it is to have your own herbs growing. So let's get started!

Chapter 1: Herbs – Uses and Benefits

Herbs have had a huge role to play in our wellbeing. They have been valued since very old times and today we depend on them all the more for cleansing our mind, body and soul. We all use herbs in our day to day life in one way or the other. Whether they bring richness to the flavour of a dish we just prepared, for healing an ailment like a flu or cough or merely for aroma, herbs are one of the most used plant types today.

With so many benefits, growing herbs at home can be truly satisfying. Herbs are commonly used in food, medicines, as pesticides and also for spiritual use. These benefits of herbs have been known and recognized world-wide and by various cultures.

Health benefits of Herbs –

- Herbs contain many essential oils, vitamins, anti-oxidants and other nutrients that can help boost our immune system. They strengthen our body and equip us to fight against germs. Some herbs that are immunity boosters are garlic, cinnamon, onion and hibiscus.

- The essential oils present in many herbs possess anti-inflammatory properties which are useful in debilitating diseases like arthritis, rheumatism, osteo-arthritis and other inflammatory conditions.

- Some of the herbs like fenugreek and bilberry have positive effects on the pancreas and hence help in stabilizing the blood sugar levels. These herbs can control type 1 and type 2 diabetes effectively. Herbs like liquorice and fenugreek also have a remarkable effect on the blood cholesterol and also the blood pressure levels.

- Herbs like Ginkgo biloba are very well known for their anti-amyloid and anti-inflammatory effects. It can effectively help in arresting the progression of Alzheimer's disease. Ginkgo biloba has been proven to be highly beneficial in Alzheimer's disease and many other forms of dementia.

- Herbs like oldenlandia and scutellaria are known to possess anti-cancer effects. Researchers have proven that these herbs can play a crucial role in treating cancer symptoms and also help in alleviating the undesirable effects of chemotherapy.

- It is a proven fact that herbs have a beneficial effect on the skin. They have been extensively used for various skin conditions. Some common herbs used for skin are neem, turmeric, basil and mint. A paste of basil, turmeric, mint and neem applied on dark spots has a lightening effect. The dark spots eventually fade away. Chamomile also has healing effects on a damaged skin. Tea tree extract is commonly seen as a vital ingredient of face washes because it has the ability to control the oil secretion from the pores.

- Healthy hair and scalp is something all of us desire. Many herbs have a vital role to play in hair care too. The extract of jojoba massaged into the scalp stimulates the growth of healthy hair. Other herbs like ginseng and marigold are also known for their role in promoting healthy growth of hair. Chamomile tea when cooled and applied to hair, acts like a natural hair toner and will give your hair a mild blonde effect too. Fenugreek helps in improving blood circulation to the hair follicles. Burdock extracts cures scalp related problems like dandruff and dryness.

- Various herbs like mint and cloves are effective in dental problems. Most of the toothpastes today speak of the role of mint and cloves in maintaining strong teeth and gums. Many herbs can be used directly on the tooth and give wonderful effects. Rubbing sage leaves on the teeth and gums cleans them instantly and smoothens their texture. Lavender water, parsley and mint can be used effectively for bad breath. Clove extracts have been used by our forefathers for toothaches. Other herbs that have a role to play in healthy gum and tooth care are fennel, neem, thyme and alpine strawberry.

- Thus we have seen that herbs have very positive effects on our body. The healing properties of various herbs vary greatly. They include carminative effects (curing gastric related problems), diaphoretic effect (controlling the water retention), analgesic effect (relieving pain), aphrodisiac effect (increasing sexual drive), antiseptic and anti-spasmodic effect.

Culinary benefits of Herbs –

Not long ago bland food was a staple food especially for people on a diet. But recent research has shown that adding some zesty herbs to tune in some flavour not only make the food palatable but also makes you healthier. Herbs add great flavour to food. They are always used in small quantities and yet add a special flavour as well as an appetizing aroma to the preparation. Some herbs also possess anti-microbial properties that keep the food protected.

It is most commonly seen that the leaf of a plant that is used for cooking is called the culinary herb and any other part of the plant used as an ingredient in the recipe (like the roots, bark, buds, flower or the stigma of the flower) are referred to as spice. Characteristically both the herbs as well as the spices are rich in antioxidants. For e.g. garlic leaves are used as herbs to add flavour to the preparation while the garlic cloves are used to give a slight pungent tinge to the food. Both the leaves and the clove of garlic are rich in antioxidants.

Some tips for using herbs in your food –

- Fresh herbs add rich flavour when sprinkled on soups or used in the preparation of various sauces

- You can use freshly chopped herbs on fruit salads and also on your sautéed or stir fried vegetables

- Herbs bring great flavour to grilled fish, chicken and other meat dishes

- Herbal leaves can also be added to some of your flavoured drinks

- Herbs protect the fatty foods from oxidation during cooking, hence it can be flawlessly paired with them to make herbed butter, herbed cheese, herbed fresh cream and also herb-infused oils

We have seen in this chapter how herbs in a small quantity impart so many benefits in therapeutically. High on antioxidants and full of flavour and aroma, herbs are versatile in every walk of life. So now that you have read about so many benefits that herbs offer, I am sure you are eager to grow them and have fresh herbs within your reach. Not only will they add greenery to your balcony of kitchen window sill or the terrace, but will also spare you the effort of going to the market specially to buy them. So let's get started! In the next chapter we will see how easy it is to grow your own fresh herbs.

Chapter 2: Growing Your Own Herbs

I am sure by now you are convinced about the benefits that herbs have to offer and that they touch our lives in one way or the other. Whether they add flavour to your food, add an aroma to your living room, make your garden or window sill look greener or even cure some of the illnesses, herbs are a part of our lives. So how do you grow them? This chapter focuses on the basic points you need to keep in mind while planting a herb garden. Follow the steps and techniques mentioned below and be rest assured that your herb garden will bloom and you will be surprised on how easily you could achieve it.

Find the perfect place to grow your herbs: Growing herbs at the right place is very important to the health of your herb plant. Some herbs bask in sunlight and flourish while others need a bit of filtered sunlight. Consider placing your herb containers in an area where you get good morning sun and filtered sunlight in the afternoon. Double check to see if the area where you have placed them receives at least 4 hours of sunlight.

Ensure each plant enjoys its space: Herbs should be placed at certain distance so as to provide them space to grow and spread. Roots are happier and healthier when they get space to spread. Sometimes you might be over-enthusiastic and might be tempted to plant as many herbs as you can in a single pot. But avoid this. Keep enough distance as plants need their own space. Also ensure that you combine those plants with similar requirements in one pot. Listed below are some general guidelines for space required by plants—

Rosemary, Mint and Oregano: 3-4 feet

Thyme, Basil and Savory: 2 feet

Chives, Dill, Parsley and Cilantro: 1 foot

Plants like mint have a frenzied growth. It quickly spreads its roots and shoots all over and needs a lot of space. Hence mint should have a pot of its own otherwise it will hamper the growth of the neighbouring plants.

Preparing the soil: You are blessed if you have a lovely garden of your own in which you can plant your herbs. Good soil is quite difficult to find and most gardeners struggle with their plants because of this. Different types of herbs can thrive in different soil conditions. By making some simple preparatory changes, you can make these soil conditions perfect for your herb plants. The soil should be well aerated and loose. Dig the soil with a gardening fork so that the water can drain out easily and the roots can easily spread down into the soil.

Regularly add compost and fertilizer to the soil and mix it well so that it is not drained out. You can use the waste vegetable peels garbage from your kitchen to make mulch. Mulch ensures that the soil remains moist and also holds on to the nutrients. Improving your garden soil is an ongoing process in gardening and can be easily achieved if you do the basics right.

Plant good quality herb plants and water them regularly: This is the final step in growing the herb. Choose what all herbs you use regularly in your daily life. Plant strong plants and see that you water them regularly. Temperature and humidity of a region plays an important role in controlling the moisture in the soil. Hence it is important that you check the soil and water it when it seems to be dry. However be careful not to over-water or it might lead to the roots to rot easily. Huge amount of water in the soil can lead to various diseases and this will in turn compromise the quality of herb you are growing.

Harvest the herb plant you have grown: When the herb has grown about 7-8 inches tall, you can simply cut off 1/3rd of its branch. Cut very close to the intersection near the lead and this will lead to faster growth of your plant. Parsley has new leaves growing from the centre. In this case cut out the oldest stalks first to clear out the way for the plant to grow further.

Be on a look out for Pests: Squirrels are such adorable animals. In fact we see such cute animations of it on kid channels. But believe me, they can be real pests. They will dig up holes in your garden completely convinced of the fact that there are acorns hidden in the soil. They will damage roots and this will affect the health of your herb plant. You can put a net around your budding plants to avoid this. Also be alert for rats and rodents who can destroy your garden in no time.

It is as simple as that! Believe me - Herbs are much easier to grow at home. All you require is a right spot which is bathed with perfect sunlight, a warm place with good soil (if growing in a garden), some containers (if growing indoors) and some good and strong plants. Growing herbs in containers is not only easy but it also saves you the time and exertion of digging up the ground to loosen the soil. But if you are one of those lucky ones who have a nice garden area and love to do gardening outdoors, then you should plant your herbs in the ground. Either ways you plant will be healthy if you diligently water the plants and regularly feed them with nutrients.

To cut the long story short, to make a simple Herb garden you will require the following:

- Some large containers or pots: these should be between 10 inches – 20 inches in diameter. You must try and grow 3-4 herbs of similar sun and water needs in one pot
- Good quality potting soil mix which is rich in compost
- Good quality Fertilizer especially organic fertilizer
- Water source

Prepare your pot by filling it with high-quality potting soil and add some fertilizer and mix it well. Moisten this mixture with some water but be careful not to over-water. Water only till the soil feels moist enough but not soggy. Now you are ready to plant your herb. Make small holes in the soil big enough to plant your herb with the roots. Now add some more soil and gently press it so that it is well supported and stands erect. Repeat for other plants. Immediately water the plant to prevent it from going dry.

Neither over-water nor under-water. Both can hamper the well-being of the plant. Ensure that your herb plants get at least 4 hours of sunlight everyday. Harvesting can be done by simply cutting $1/3^{rd}$ of the branch so that you plant regrows nicely. There you are! Your herb garden is ready. That was simple, isn't it? So what are you waiting for? Go ahead and try and experience the rewards!

Chapter 3: Common Herbs and their Care

I am sure by now you are already convinced that herbs are the most rewarding container as well as garden crops. They are very easy to grow and require minimum effort. A friend of mine has a beautiful herb garden of her own and she was sharing with me that there are 2 important things one should practice while growing a herb garden. Firstly, you must pick up the herbs when it is the season and be sure not to break the main stem. This will encourage your plants to grow tall and gangly. Secondly, feeding your herbs with seaweeds will provide good nutrition to your herbs and they will be richer in aroma and flavour.

There are a variety of herbs that exist, but I am going to talk about the commonly used ones that are easy to grow. These herbs will require minimum effort and time and you can grow them in your garden or in containers.

Basil:

If you are a novice, start with basil. Basil is a herb used in almost various recipes. It is the best thing that a new gardener can grow as it is very encouraging to see it grow without much effort or care. It is easy to understand its watering patterns as basil will show you when it lacks water. It will wilt and look gloomy. The moment you water it, within minutes it will perk up. Basil should always be cut from the top.

Snip the stem right above the place where you see baby leaves coming out. These will grow into new stems and spread. Never pluck leaves from the bottom. The lower leaves are the source of solar power for the plant. This will make your plant look bushier. Also remember to snip off the flower buds before they bloom so that you encourage growth of new branch stems. Basil plant roots from a cutting. Place the stem cutting in water for a few days and you will see it rooting. Once the roots are an inch long, you can plant it in soil and watch it grow.

Uses: Basil gives a spicy flavour and also a lovely aroma when added to soups and stir-fry. Use it liberally in your sauces, soups, salads and omelettes. Basil is also used as a medicine for coughs and colds. A concoction of basil, honey and lemon juice helps in coughs and cold.

Coriander:

Coriander is mostly planted in spring. Once planted it grows quickly and flowers in no time. If you live in an area where spring is for a short time, then try planting it in rich soil, in a shady place and where you can use it regularly. You can plan to sow coriander seeds in August or September. You will start seeing them sprout and also see the leaves by autumn. Once well-established, they continue to grow well in winters and then in spring you can have them flourishing and blooming all the more.

Uses: Dry coriander seeds are used in cooking various vegetarian and non-vegetarian dishes. Coriander leaves are used to garnish various dishes and is widely used in all countries across cultures. The young baby leaves of coriander are also referred to as cilantro. Coriander roots are known to possess medicinal values.

Mint:

Mint, as discussed earlier, is an excellent and rewarding container plant. Once planted it grows like wild. Mint needs regular watering and nutrient supply. Feed it well and see it flourish. Once your plant has grown into a bush, remove it from the container, split it into quarters and replant it in other pots. You will have a mint farm of your own before you know. Mint has many varieties. Some are used to flavour tea and some are used in cooking.

Uses: Mint gives a strong flavour to mojitos, chutneys, meat gravies and tea. Mint is also used as a main ingredient in mint sauce. While marinating meats, sprinkle and rub fresh mint all over. This gives an appetizing flavour to your dish.

Chives:

Chives are both, full of flavour and also beautiful to look at when they flower. You can easily grow them on your window sill or along a garden fence to add some splendour and flavour. The flowers are very attractive and bloom in the spring. They taste possess a lip-smacking taste and attract bees. Chives mostly need minimum 4-5 hours of sunlight. Make sure you keep the soil damp by watering it regularly.

Uses: Chives have a mild onion-like flavour. They are used liberally in soups, salads and go well with mashed potatoes. Various sandwich spreads and sauces also contain chives. Flowers can be used in salads and add a lot of colour to your food, making it look palatable.

Dill:

The best way to grow dill is by planting seeds and watching them germinate. They are quick and easy to grow with good sunlight and water. Using mulch in the soil helps as it retains the necessary moisture for the plants. Dill grows well in tropical areas. Dill flowers add a lot of beauty to your garden and attract butterflies too. It is an easy backyard vegetable too. Dill plant also attracts other advantageous insects like wasps and predatory insects to your garden.

To ensure a good crop, continue sowing the seeds every few weeks. This way you will get a continued harvest throughout the growing season. If you have a variety of vegetables in your garden, you can plant dill next to cabbage, onions and even garlic. But avoid planting it next to carrots.

Uses: Dill is commonly used in pickles, soups, pastas and stews. Dill seeds and leaves have a strong bitter taste. You can use dill to flavour a cucumber salad or even add it to your

Rosemary:

Rosemary contains a compound called carnosic acid which in a way helps in fighting against cancer. It needs a lot of sunshine and should be watered frequently. It possesses a strong and fragrant aroma which is released even if you touch it.

Use soil that is rich in compost and adding mulch over the soil helps as this plant needs moisture all the time. However ensure that the soil is well-drained too much watering can disease its roots. Rather than seed, I would recommend that you grow Rosemary using a seedling or with a cutting of the plant that is established. This will increase the chances of its survival.

Uses: Owing to its fragrance, rosemary is used in various soups, breads, biscuits, meat stock and a variety of other recipes. Rosemary essential oil when used with various base oils like almond oil or olive oil offers a wide array of health benefits. Rosemary oil helps in ailments like indigestion, stress and also helps in boosting immunity. It is also widely used in skin and hair care products.

Thyme:

It is a bit tough to grow thyme and you have to be patient as it is really slow at germinating. If you are the impatient variety, plant seedlings or cuttings in a well drained soil. This herb grows with small and attractive purple flowers. You can grow it for its medicinal and culinary uses and also to rev up the look of you backyard, balcony, garden or your window. Thyme needs sunlight but it shouldn't be too strong.

It can also be planted indoors because it does not grow tall. It will concise itself to the pot in which it is planted. So plant it in places where you get good sunlight and preferably in a container. Once the plant flowers, do remember to prune it. This will encourage its growth. Also every season divide the plant and re-pot it and see how it flourishes.

Uses: Thyme helps in alleviating the symptoms of bronchitis and other respiratory disorders. It also possesses antiseptic properties. It is also used in soups and salads. Guess what, it is used to flavour champagne too!

Sage:

You can grow sage by buying seeds and planting them. However like other herbs, it is best to take cuttings from an established plant or buy seedlings and plant them in your garden. It is perennial and a very hardy plant that needs no fuss. Be sure to keep watering the young plants and also prune the grown ones on regular basis. Sage has a variety of flowers – pink, purple, blue or even white. Sage needs full sunlight for at least 5-6 hours. Preferably use loamy soil (soil containing a good proportion of sand. silt and clay).

If you have many other plants and herbs, plant a sage next to rosemary, carrot or cabbage. Avoid planting sage near cucumber as sage impacts the taste and the growth of cucumber. During the first year when your plant grows, avoid harvesting it completely so as to ensure that your plant becomes bushier and grows fully. When you prune it, do so along with the woody stems.

Uses: Sage has a long history of medicinal and culinary benefit. Just like rosemary and other herbs, sage contains volatile essential oils that are well-known for their health benefits. The meaning of the word 'sage' is wise and true to its name, it helps improve brain function. Sage possesses antioxidant properties that helps improve cognition.

Patients with Alzheimer's disease and Parkinson's disease are advised to include sage in their diet through soups, stir fry vegetables or sandwiches. Sages tastes best when it is fresh. However you can sundry it and store it in your freezer for use later. Sage is lavishly used in cooking and in various stuffings.

Lavender:

Compared to other herbs, lavender is larger and should be grown outdoors, preferably should be planted in the ground. It needs at least eight hours of sunlight everyday of make sure you place it in an area that is sunlit adequately. It needs well-drained soil. You can mix the soil with builder's sad to improve the drainage.

In case you are thinking of planting it indoors to add beauty to your living room, make sure the container in which it is planted has many holes. This will help the water to drain out of the soil. Keep adding compost and organic matter to the soil at regular intervals. This will enhance the aroma and improve the quality of the herb. Prune the stalks in spring or during its harvest time and regularly trim it if you do not want a tall plant. The soil pH is very crucial while growing lavender. Ensure that the soil is alkaline with a pH between 6.5-7.5.

Uses: Lavender is a very pretty plant with lavender flowers and is very aromatic. It is packed with a lot of health benefits. The lavender aroma is strongly fragrant and soothing. The essential oils extracted from Lavender helps in relieving stress and is used in cases of insomnia. Lavender is rich in antioxidants and is beneficial in cases of belly bloating. Lavender is more of a soothing herb and is used in cases of agitation related to dementia, nervousness and restlessness. It is also used to cure cuts, wounds, earaches, eczema and burns. The lavender blooms when dried can be used to make a calming tea concoction.

Parsley:
Just like thyme, parsley will test your patience as they are very slow to catch up and grow. But once they do, they will reap you benefits for at least 2 years before they flower and wilt away.

Parsley grows well when planted in moist soil that is rich in compost. Parsley requires regular watering in order to encourage tap root development. Unlike basil, parsley rarely recovers once it wilts. So regular watering is a must. A variety of weeds easily blend with parsley and may hamper its growth. Hence ensure you do away with these weeds at regular intervals.

Uses: Parsley is commonly used for garnishing and flavouring many dishes. It eliminated bad breath and hence can be chewed on to refresh your breath. Parsley is rich in Vitamin A, C and K and hence should be included in diet.

These were some most common herbs that you can grow at home and reap benefits. I am sure by now you are confident of growing them. Start small and work towards adding more herbs to your garden and see them flourishing with the necessary care.

Chapter 4: Some Quick Tips

By now you may of thought of various options on the layout and the design of your garden. You may be having a rough idea on whether you want a full-fledged garden or a container garden close to your kitchen or in your balcony. Before you start here are some concluding quick tips that you must keep in mind while planting your own herb garden.

Plant seedlings instead of seeds:

As a novice at growing herbs, it would be more encouraging to plant a seedling instead of waiting for a seed to sprout. It is indeed a rewarding experience to see a seeds germinate and grow into plants. However it's not worth all the effort as you don't want to waste time in your busy schedule waiting for the entire process. Instead of that, visit a good nursery or a market and buy established seedlings, plant it in your garden and watch them grow. You will see great results with minimum effort rather than getting discouraged with sprouts which take a long time and also have a high chance of dying away.

Consider how much sunlight your garden gets:

As discussed earlier, most plants and herbs need at least 4 hours of sunlight. Consider a location which receives a balance of bright morning sun and filtered afternoon sun. Some locations are blocked by either a structure or a large tree. Avoid setting up your garden in these areas. You will learn more about which location is suitable for your herbs once your keep a track during the course of the day on how much sunlight is received, till what time and when it leaves. Also take the various seasons into consideration. During summers the sunrays are harsh and in winter you plants might receive very less sunlight.

Be sure that your garden is protected:

Avoid planting your garden along a walkway or a fire exit. Not only is it dangerous but also can harm your plants in case of an emergency. Place your garden or herb containers in a place that is clear of any mess or isn't coming in the way of a regular path. Also be on a look out for rodents and squirrels who can mess up your garden within minutes.

Remember to put plants that go well together:

Do you like salsa sauce? Grow tomatoes, peppers and cilantro in your garden. There are more chances of them being consumed early. Avoid growing things that you don't use often or they will just remain like untidy bushes in your garden.

Conclusion

So are you ready for action? You have come this far reading this article, means that you have followed the tips and techniques shared in this article and are highly motivated and ready to grow your own herb garden. Growing herbs in your backyard is quite exciting and a money-saving leisure pursuit. Having a handy garden of herbs helps you take advantage of the heath and culinary benefits that they have to offer. That too, fresh herbs!

Through the article you may also have learnt that growing herbs does not take much but you will definitely be paid back a huge bonus. Research has proven that as time passes the nutritional value of herbs reduces. Growing fresh herbs offers you more nutrition as it is just fresh from your garden. You will experience the benefits only when you start off and believe me, its worth all your time and effort. Whether you own an acre of land or have just a backyard or a balcony to spare.

If you are interested and motivated enough you will start the process today. Just narrow down the herbs you most commonly use in your cooking and include them in your garden. When you feel you are not doing too well, don't be low. Just remind yourself of the various benefits you will accrue. When you feel the push for including more herbs, just do it. After all if you don't experiment you will never learn!

I am sure, this article that I have written, has motivated you and provided you with the knowledge needed to grow your own herbs. So flavour up your dishes and liven up your lifestyle by following the various tips share in this article. Amy your herbs grow and spread their aroma in your lives!

Printed in Great Britain
by Amazon